BRITAIN IN OLD PHO

Eastbourne Past & Present

DAVID ARSCOTT

SUTTON PUBLISHING

Sutton Publishing Limited
Phoenix Mill · Thrupp · Stroud
Gloucestershire · GL5 2BU

First published 2001

Copyright © David Arscott, 2001

Title page photograph: Terminus Road,
c. 1935.

British Library Cataloguing in Publication Data
A catalogue record for this book is available from the
British Library.

ISBN 0-7509-2781-X

Typeset in 10.5/13.5 Photina.
Typesetting and origination by
Sutton Publishing Limited.
Printed and bound in England by
J.H. Haynes & Co. Ltd, Sparkford.

4 Elms Buildings, Seaside Road, *c.* 1902. A fitting salutation to begin the book, but a curiosity, too. The so-called Christian Waiters' Club and registry office shared this building, which has long since disappeared.

CONTENTS

Eastbourne Gas Company was formed in 1851, with the gasworks close to the railway station. Its offices and showroom in Terminus Road are here seen 'dressed overall' for the coronation of Edward VII.

INTRODUCTION

O n the face of it Eastbourne should have changed rather less than most towns since its major development from four small and separate settlements around the middle of the nineteenth century. After all, the 7th Duke of Devonshire (the prime, but not the sole, mover in this process) was at great pains to build this 'Empress of Watering Places' on the grand scale, with impressive villas fronting tree-lined avenues which had a look of luxurious permanence from the outset.

To ensure the lasting elegance of the long seafront with its tiered promenades, moreover, he had covenants drawn up to prevent the spread of the sort of gimcrack novelty shops and ice-cream kiosks which make (according to taste) a delightful or tone-lowering contribution to the ambience of the archetypal English seaside resort.

Although a good deal of the elegance remains, and although very little commercial 'tat' has forced its way on to the seafront, the photographs in this book nevertheless reveal extensive changes to Eastbourne over the years. Many of them reflect nothing more than what is lazily referred to as progress – the ever-evolving needs of a growing population. Old buildings can sometimes no longer be satisfactorily adapted to the uses now required of them, and (unless they are masterpieces) their replacement is desirable as well as inevitable.

Other changes had a more dramatic cause: German bombs. Outside London, no town in the south east of England suffered more from enemy air raids during the last war, with 200 people losing their lives in them. The effect on the townscape was stark: around 500 houses were destroyed, with another thousand seriously damaged. The Langney Road/Bourne Street area was so regularly targeted, and so cruelly devastated, that it became known to locals as Hell Fire Corner.

As one might expect, the buildings which rose from the ashes of these vicious attacks were variable in quality. It is, however, all too easy to compare an unsurprising modern reality with a 'charming' postcard view. Some of the contrasts in these pages are, indeed, brutal but this is not a depressing book overall. To many of its inhabitants, and to the crowds who flock here in the holiday season, the old 'Empress' has successfully adapted to her modern role, rather like those Scandinavian monarchs who get about on bicycles. Originally built 'by gentlemen for gentlemen', Eastbourne is now Everyman's watering place.

Those four early settlements which eventually fused and were swallowed by modern Eastbourne were Bourne (now the Old Town), Southbourne (the South Street/Grove

Road area), Sea Houses (the eastern part of the seafront now known as Marine Parade) and Meads.

In 1801 there were but 243 houses and 1,700 inhabitants in all four hamlets. The town's sudden growth was stimulated by the craze for healthy sea bathing and by the arrival of the railway in 1849. Terminus Road, leading from the new station to the seafront, was laid over a muddy track to the sea as early as 1850.

It was in 1858, however, that money began to speak. In that year the 7th Duke of Devonshire (William Cavendish, Earl of Burlington) inherited his title and became one of the richest men in England. In furtherance of his dream he now sent his architect, Henry Currey, on a tour of Europe to bring back ideas that would make his new resort the finest in Britain.

The 80ft wide boulevard of Devonshire Place was merely the grandest of many fine avenues. With hotels and mansions springing up along and behind the seafront, the population had risen to 22,000 by 1881 and was still climbing rapidly. Two years later the town's local board applied for a charter of incorporation, and the borough of Eastbourne was created – still, it must be said, grateful for Cavendish patronage, but on its way to bringing the town genuine self-government. The extravagant town hall on the site of the former village stocks in Grove Road was completed in 1886, opening to the proud strains of the Hallelujah Chorus.

Ocklynge Mill, 1925. This tower mill, which once stood on the western side of the A22, was blown up in the 1930s.

Any town which creates a by-law prohibiting barking by dogs holds itself up to ridicule, and this cartoonist duly obliged. With its ducal origins, Eastbourne has always had something of a 'superior' reputation.

There will be a very few readers who know their Eastbourne so well that each photograph, old and new, will immediately cry out its location. I worked in the town for several years, running the BBC's local radio studio in Gildredge Road, and so came to acquire a fairly good 'furriner's' feel for it. Enlisting the help of knowledgeable locals (*see page 128*) has nevertheless proved invaluable. Many buildings have disappeared altogether, while others have left fragmentary traces which one discovers with a silent Eureka!

To give a workable structure for those who wish to visit the places pictured here, I have divided the town into a number of convenient sectors – and had better apologise straight away to those living in suburban Eastbourne for the fact that the book seldom strays very far from the areas in and between those original four hamlets. The photographic record is, for obvious reasons, much more detailed here.

We begin at the railway station, and turn briefly west to take in the end of Upperton Road and the Avenue, with a glance up Grove Road on the way. Returning to Terminus Road, we then take in the modern shopping centre, where traces of the old townscape can still be found, if sometimes well hidden.

Our third excursion takes us to the town hall in Grove Road and then down South Street, with brief excursions to either side, while the seafront fittingly commandeers the central, and longest, part of the book – from the western lawns by way of the Grand, Marine and Royal Parades to the Redoubt fortress. The changes here are more subtle, since the grander buildings have generally stood the test of time, but the contrasts between having a good time then and now are fascinating to observe.

For our fifth stroll we begin at Trinity Trees, near the war memorial, and proceed along Seaside Road and Seaside (neither of which is beside the sea), stepping aside from this long thoroughfare occasionally to look into Susans Road, Pevensey Road and Cavendish Place.

The Old Town is our sixth area. It has seen more change than it ought, but retains some notable buildings (the church, the Old Parsonage and the Lamb Inn among them) as well as Motcombe Gardens – its pond fed by the stream which gives the town its name.

We next visit the Meads, otherwise known as 'the Belgravia of Eastbourne' (planned by Currey in 1872 as an exclusive area and arguably living up to its ideal better than any other part of the town) before ending our visual tour with a brief visit to the town's extremities, west and east.

I have attempted for the most part to take today's photographs from the same standpoint as the 'then' shots, although on some occasions a sense of self-preservation has made this difficult on our traffic-crowded roads. Since they are themselves a historical record, however humble, I should add that they were all taken in July and August 2001. Anyone repeating the exercise a hundred years from now will doubtless find changes every bit as great as I have encountered, and my hope for Eastbourne is that most of them will be for the betterment of this splendid seaside town.

David Arscott
November, 2001

1

Around the Station

Station and Terminus Road, *c.* 1905.

There have been four successive railway stations at Eastbourne, and this photograph shows the unpretentious second phase. The first was little more than a wooden hut.

The station in its third phase, *c.* 1905, looking much as it does today.

Today's view is inevitably partly obscured by an array of traffic signals, but the station is clearly well cared for and the flowers along the front are an attractive touch. The London, Brighton and South Coast Railway extended the railway from Polegate to Eastbourne in 1849, so enabling the development of the resort planned by the Duke of Devonshire and the other major local landowners, the Gilbert family.

57   *EASTBOURNE. — Interior of the Railway Station. — LL.*

Station interior *c.* 1906. A wonderful view, full of detail, with advertisers leaving few areas of brickwork uncovered. Everyone is wearing a hat.

In with modern gadgetry and out with all that advertising, although the potted palm in the foreground is perhaps a subtle form of it: seaside resorts like to grow exotics as a badge of their balmy climate.

Where the engine sheds with their turntable once stood, north of the station (above), there is now the Enterprise Shopping Centre. This is a completely new building, but it carries a pleasing echo of its predecessor, something planners might perhaps attempt more often.

Terminus Road *c.* 1920. The identical view to page 9, but with cars and a bus now making an appearance. The Gildredge Hotel on the left beyond the station was badly damaged by a German bomb in November, 1940.

Today's view is similar, with a less imposing Gildredge Hotel in place of the original.

These shots show no architectural changes between the late 1960s and today, but the positioning of the bus-stop is a testimony to the relentless increase in traffic. Buses can no longer park outside the station, leaving the traffic free to flow to the left down Ashford Road. Note the 'low floor' bus in the modern picture – easier for older folk and parents with pushchairs to get on and off.

Upperton Road, *c.* 1910. The station is behind us in this tranquil scene. This postcard was sent to a man in Lyon, France, by his young niece Marie, who marked her school (right of picture) with a cross. We shall see it in more detail in page 18.

Deep Pan Pizza now occupies the ground floor of the large building to the left, where previously there were shops selling leather goods and confectionery. The new post office, built in 1915, can be seen in the centre of the picture.

The Technical Institute and Free Library, Grove Road, 1904. The 8th Duke of Devonshire donated the site for this prestigious building in 1899, and the nature of the gathering outside it suggests that this was the opening ceremony on 8 August 1904. The building was destroyed by enemy action on 4 June 1943, when no fewer than 18 aircraft bombed the town.

Eastbourne had to wait more than 20 years for its new library, a building which speaks of its time. It was opened on 6 April 1964.

Girls' secondary school, Upperton Road, *c.* 1935. Here is the back of the school we mentioned on page 16. It looks substantial here, but former pupils remember its being a wellworn place before the outbreak of war, and some years later it was pulled down.

Caffyns garage (also seen from the rear) now occupies the site.

Upperton Road Maternity Home, 1997. Next door to the girls' school was this nursing home, which lasted rather longer. Many an Eastbournian was born here in the days before hospital birth for almost all, and the mother of three of them took this photograph when she knew that its days were numbered.

'It was a wonderful friendly place to have your baby. All babies were in a big light airy nursery situated at the back of the building, looked after by the nursery nurses (yellow uniform). We were all allowed in the nursery at any time, but babies only came out into the wards at feed times.'

The occupants are somewhat older now that Bovis have developed the site as retirement apartments.

The Avenue. These two pictures, about a century apart, show little basic change, although the road has been widened considerably. The horse-drawn bus in the old picture is, characteristically, plastered with advertisements.

2

The Shopping Centre

Home & Colonial Stores, Terminus Road, *c.* 1905. What a forgotten era is hinted at in that name, harking back to the days when there was an empire to run and many boarding schools in Sussex were filled with children whose parents were far away doing just that.

Terminus Road, *c.* 1925. The railway station determined where the shopping centre of Eastbourne would quickly develop. This picture shows the Lewes Old Bank on the left. To the left ran Junction Road, which was swallowed up when the Arndale Centre was developed. The bank was destroyed in a German bombing raid in March 1943.

Royal Hotel, Terminus Road, *c.* 1925. A closer view of the Royal Hotel, which can be seen behind the trees in the top picture.

The view today of what is known as Bankers' Corner. The Lewes Old Bank has been replaced by the Terminus branch of Barclays, while the Royal Hotel has given way to the NatWest Bank.

A ninety degree turn from the above, with the entrance of Barclays Bank on the right and Sussex Stationers on the left. Next to it is one of the entrances to the Arndale Centre, opened in November 1980. The clearing of the site necessitated the demolition not only of Junction Road, but of Terminus Place, part of Tideswell Road and many small shops.

Terminus Road, *c.* 1920. A view towards the station, with Cornfield Road on the left.

The buildings on the left are largely unchanged today, but this part of the road is now reserved for buses and delivery vans.

Town crier, *c.* 1905. The borough has no official post, but Eastbourne has had three commercial town criers, and here is the first of them – Clement Reed. He died at the age of 57 after falling from a bus in the Goffs.

Tony Chamberlain-Brothers is today's incumbent, a natural showman willing to don the gear and bend the ear of the milling crowd – 'It's a kind of theatre. I push myself on the public, but they enjoy it or I wouldn't do it.' He is seen here ringing the opening of the T.J. Hughes store, formerly the Army and Navy, in Terminus Road.

Sussex Gardens, yesterday and today. You'll search in vain in this 1920s picture (above) for the shop which once had 10 Sussex Gardens as its address, but the sign on the pillar in Terminus Road has the clue. A handsome terrace lay well back from a service road here before the development of the Arndale Centre, and the roofs and upper storeys of the houses can still be seen behind and above the present shop frontages.

Sussex Gardens/Terminus Road. Most of the classical features here have disappeared, but a few remain as a reminder of past glories.

A new look indeed, but there's an echo of the buildings which stood here before. See, for instance, the gas company showroom on page 4.

Today Terminus Road is pedestrianised between Cornfield Road and Bolton Road, with the Arndale Centre on the left.

YMCA headquarters, Langney Road, *c.* 1922. The size of the building and the large number of people crammed into these excursion coaches would suggest a thriving organisation.

A central section of the terrace has been replaced, and now the shopper is king. On the left of the picture is a building we shall meet again on page 87.

3

The South Street Area

Princess Alice's Tree and South Street, *c.* 1910.

The town hall from South Street, *c.* 1910. The clock tower rises 130 ft, and contains a one-ton bell and four smaller ones. The magnificent town hall at the top of Grove Road, built in red brick and dressed with Portland stone, was completed in 1886 at the then very considerable cost of £40,000.

The road is now one-way to traffic. At the far end a sign proclaims that the array of smart shops in this area now likes to be known as 'Little Chelsea'.

Proclamation of George V, 1910. The Duke of Devonshire, as Mayor of Eastbourne, is here seen reading the proclamation of the king from the town hall balcony at noon on 9 May 1910. The Eastbourne Municipal Orchestra waits to strike up a fanfare.

The town hall today. On the right is a newly-completed ramp to allow wheelchairs into the reception area of the building.

Grange Road, *c.* 1905. The town hall is the focal point in this view, which shows the road densely lined with trees.

Today there are far fewer trees. The wall on the right fronts Eastbourne College, 'a school for the sons of gentlemen' which opened in 1867 on land donated by the Duke of Devonshire.

South Street, *c.* 1900. The tower of St Saviour's Church is a regular landmark in views of South Street, this picture being taken from a little in front of the town hall. The lettering on the wall on the left proclaims West End Registry Office and (above the awning) A. Store, Fruiterer. On the right is the New Inn Tap.

Praise be for continuity: the more substantial building on the right remains the New Inn, 'established in 1880', although it has been extended further towards the town hall. Modern council offices have replaced the Townsend store on the left, but the building which houses the registry office is still there, behind the Little Chelsea sign.

Gildredge Road, 1930. This card was produced to advertise 'The Laurels', a boarding establishment halfway down Gildredge Road between South Street and the station.

The building looks better cared for today, but several of its grace notes have gone. The windows of the solicitors' office have lost their attractive iron grilles, and the small gardens and their fronting walls have been completely stripped away.

South Street, looking west from Gildredge Road. Only the bend in the road survives to suggest that these two views were from the same spot. The top picture dates from around 1870, before the town hall rose above the skyline in the distance.

South Street. The street number is the only clue to what has replaced the Alfred Wright & Sons antiques shop in South Street. (The advertising card boasts 'reasonable prices', adding 'all goods marked in plain figures'.) It wasn't a thing of beauty, but it was certainly more attractive than its successor, which is now home to the solicitors Hurst, Reade.

South Street and St Saviour's Church from Cornfield Road. A century separates these two photographs, and yet the buildings are largely the same. The road is now one-way towards the church, and certainly is no longer suitable for strolling along. St Saviour's was consecrated in 1872, and after a thanksgiving service the vicar climbed the tower to install a weathervane on the top.

Princess Alice's Tree, *c.* 1906. This view is taken from the end of Devonshire Place, with Cornfield Road in the background and South Street (obscured from view) leading off to the left. The tree in the centre was planted by Princess Alice, the second daughter of Queen Victoria, on one of her visits to Eastbourne for her health. She died at the age of 35.

The layout has of course changed to accommodate modern traffic, with a large roundabout in the centre, but the chief difference between the two pictures is that the princess's tree has gone and been replaced by the war memorial. It was raised in 1920 to honour the 1,056 local men and women killed in the First World War.

4

The Seafront

Sea Houses, *c.* 1870.

Western Lawns, *c.* 1920. The 'fashion' used to parade on the lawns at the beginning of Grand Parade. It was a good place to see and be seen, and popular with young people hoping to meet a suitable partner. The Wish Tower, one of a chain built to deter Napoleonic invasion, can be seen in the distance.

Dress is informal today, and the crowds who attend regular events on the lawns during the season expect to eat on the hoof – something that would have been frowned upon all those years ago. The vans here are selling chips, ice cream, doughnuts and crêpes.

A close-up of the statue of the 8th Duke of Devonshire suffering some indignity on the Western Lawns. The statue was unveiled by the Duke of Norfolk in October 1910, with the then Duke of Devonshire in attendance.

Grand Hotel, *c.* 1915. The lawns face the magnificent Grand Hotel, built in 1876. The Edwardian age had just passed at the time this picture was taken, but the women's clothes display the characteristic elegance. 'Aunt Doll', who sent this postcard to her nephew in 1915, has marked her room with the regulation cross.

A very tall children's slide at the event pictured on page 40 provided a view that is today impossible from the lawns because of the mature shrubs and trees. The composer Claud Debussy, who wrote part of *La Mer* while staying here, is one of countless 'names' who have patronised the five-star hotel. The BBC once regularly broadcast performances by the Palm Court Orchestra from the Grand.

Lifeboat house, *c.* 1904. The legacy of James Stevens of Birmingham allowed 20 lifeboats to be launched in Britain, and this is the *James Stevens No. 6*, which arrived here in October, 1899. The boathouse had been opened below the Wish Tower in July the previous year, after the *Daily Telegraph* raised a fund to pay for it in memory of the actor William Terriss – assassinated outside the stage door of the Adelphi Theatre, London.

The lifeboat house went out of service in 1924, the *James Stevens* having by then been launched forty-three times and saved thirty-four lives. The building reopened as a museum in 1937, while the lifeboat, when it was replaced, has a new life as a pleasure boat taking people round the lighthouse.

Wish Tower slopes, *c*. 1890. A wall by the Wish Tower has several Victorian plates set into it, bearing the letters GCS, BCS, HCS and SPS. The first of them refers to the goat chaise stands once licensed on the spot, and here are two of the young lads who plied for hire, their badges of authority slung over their shoulders. (The other plates signify bath chair stand, hackney carriage stand and saddled pony stand.)

The pier at this stage is almost bare apart from the theatre at its seaward end. Another major contrast between old and new photographs is the uncompromising modern building on the left. The Mayfair Hotel gave way to the Transport and General Workers' Union holiday and conference centre in 1976.

Beach and Grand Parade, *c.* 1910. Suntan lotion would surely have had few takers in a population which dressed up so thoroughly even in the best of weather. Here we see some of the bathing machines presumably newly arrived, since the horses are still in the shafts. What they contributed to the quality of the bathing water one doesn't care to imagine.

Neat rows of changing huts have replaced their colourful predecessors, although there are still a few wheels on the beach. Note the incursion of an ice cream kiosk on the once-unsullied foreshore. A sign of things to come?

Looking west to the Wish Tower. There are more buildings today, albeit of a relatively flimsy nature, but the changes over nearly a century (the postcard was sent in 1908) are relatively slight. The elegance has certainly departed, and we have no need today of the notice about public bathing seen in the shrubbery on the right of the picture.

17 Wilmington Square, 1909. 'This is our house, so you can see there is plenty to do,' wrote the sender of this card. Wilmington Square runs down from Grand Parade near the Wish Tower towards the Congress Theatre and is today beautifully maintained, with central gardens which were given to the council by the Chatsworth Estate in 1949. Early photographs show the gardens divided by hedges, whereas today it is an open space with paths winding among flower beds. Note the raised passageway linking one of the seafront buildings to another behind it.

No longer end-of-terrace, No. 17 has become attached to an expanding Wish Tower Hotel so that the once open passage between the buildings is now partly covered. Clearly, plenty has been done!

Entrance to Devonshire Park, *c.* 1905. The town's first entertainments centre was developed on this site in the 1870s, comprising a pavilion, a theatre, a racquets court and a splendid floral hall (or winter garden) of glass and iron where daily concerts were given during the season. The first demonstration of electric lighting in Eastbourne was staged here in July 1881, a local paper enthusing that 'the Floral Hall – like a miniature Crystal palace – wore the appearance of one of the enchanted palaces to be read of in the Arabian Nights'. In 1875 the inventor of the roller skate, J.C. Plimpton, gave a demonstration to open a huge new indoor and outdoor rink.

The glass has gone from the roof and the palm trees and other exotica from inside, but the Grade II listed Winter Garden is still very much alive as an entertainments venue, hosting exhibitions, dinners and dances.

Indian Pavilion, Devonshire Park, *c.* 1910. The Royal Naval Exhibition at Chelsea first saw this oriental fantasy, the so-called Indian Pavilion. After gracing that event in 1897 it was dismantled and reassembled in Devonshire Park, where it was used as dressing rooms and to serve refreshments.

The Congress Theatre, not seen at its best from within the park, was built here in 1963, and the Indian Pavilion had to make way for it. The first South of England tennis championships were held in the park in 1881, and Devonshire Park is today one of the country's top venues.

Devonshire Park Theatre, *c.* 1910. The Italianate style of the theatre's towers was the work of the Duke of Devonshire's architect Henry Currey, but the towers themselves were more than ornaments. Mindful of fires at several London theatres in the recent past, Currey built fire-proof emergency staircases into them, and set large water tanks attached to hydrants at the top. The theatre opened on 2 June 1884. A sign directs upper circle clientele to the main entrance, with those using the 'pit and gallery' being pointed to a side door.

The original interior was much altered by Frank Matcham in 1903 (and to great acclaim), but the outside remains much as it was. Nowadays there are far fewer billboards outside, and everyone uses the same entrance.

The beach, *c.* 1910. This photograph is taken below Devonshire Place, with the so-called birdcage bandstand in the centre and the Cavendish Hotel on the left. In such fine weather the children are allowed to take off their shoes and socks.

A woman washes sand from her legs before the long trek over the shingle. Taking photographs seems more intrusive today, when holidaymakers are much more scantily clad.

The Cavendish Hotel. Named for the town's foremost land-owning family, the dukes of Devonshire, this imposing hotel opened in 1873. The older picture shows it before a Messerschmitt attack on the afternoon of 4 May 1942, which destroyed the east wing – second time unlucky, for an earlier bomb had lodged itself in a wall but failed to explode.

Today's photograph shows that the perennial struggle between restoration and renewal was on this occasion won by the modernisers.

Devonshire Place, *c.* 1910. The statue of the 7th Duke was erected by public subscription in 1901 at the seaward end of the town's grandest boulevard. The road was originally intended to stretch as far as the railway station.

The new wing of the Cavendish Hotel protrudes on the left, some of the mansions have been replaced by blocks of flats and there are fewer trees, yet Devonshire Place still makes an impact today.

Birdcage bandstand, *c.* 1901. We have met this little bandstand before (page 53) and now see it more closely. It was built in 1882 and stood just off the Lower Parade on cast-iron stilts.

Here is its replacement, the Central Bandstand, its confident curves declaring its age: it was built in 1935. Considerably larger than its predecessor, it can seat 3,000 people and is protected from the weather by glass screens.

Listening to the band, *c.* 1910 and 2001 – a lasting pleasure. Eastbourne was the first British seaside resort to have its own symphony orchestra, and one of its members is honoured on a plaque on a bandstand wall. John Wesley Woodward, who played in the Eastbourne Municipal Orchestra, the Duke of Devonshire's Orchestra and the Grand Hotel Orchestra, was a member of the ship's orchestra on board the Titanic when it sank on 15 April 1912.

The beach, *c.* 1905. 'This is a nice place,' wrote the sender of this view of the beach looking towards a still largely undeveloped pier. As so often, there is a good crop of colourful wheeled bathing machines, but no sign of any eagerness actually to get into the sea.

With the tide further out than in the older photograph, everyone is taking advantage of the sea and sand – and probably getting a little burned into the bargain.

Lower Parade, *c.* 1905. The windscreen along the pier was erected in 1902–3, which helps date this picture. In the foreground a man appears to be making a purchase, perhaps of fish or shellfish.

There's a customer in just about the same place in the recent picture, but today's purchase is ice cream.

The pier. As one might expect, the pier has changed considerably since it was first opened on 13 June 1870. Designed by that most famous of pier architects, Eugenius Birch, it was at first little more than a promenade deck, with attractive little kiosks at the landward end. The top picture of around 1895 shows the theatre which was built at the far end in 1888, and which served its purpose until 1899. The lower photograph, looking the other way, reemphasises the lack of clutter on the pier. Were those rowing boats for hire?

The pier, *c.* 1905. The seaward end is much the same, but this photograph shows the new theatre erected in 1899. The dome contained a camera obscura, projecting a picture of the area all round the pier, and the new complex included a bar, a café and the pier offices. In 1901 two games saloons were erected halfway along the deck, and these can be clearly seen, too.

Looks familiar? The pier entrance was changed in 1912, the original kiosks being replaced by taller affairs with cupolas (see page 63). The small central kiosk was first removed to Gildredge Park, where it was used by the bowling club. Late in 1994 it found its way to the Redoubt Gardens (above), where it is now an ice cream kiosk. Here we see workmen finishing the job.

The pier, *c.* 1908. The games saloons are in place on either side of the pier, and the original kiosks still stand by the entrance. The skittish seaside architecture extends to the domed shelter in the centre of the photograph and the embellishments atop the windbreak of glass and iron.

The similar view today is rather more prosaic, though not without its playful touches.

The pier, *c.* 1934. Here are the kiosks erected in 1912, but a new pavilion has been built over a large area of the
pier. 'What a nice place this is,' writes the sender of this postcard.

The entrance has changed yet again, but the kiosk theme has been retained.

The pier today. Roller skates are a popular form of locomotion along the seafront at the beginning of the twenty-first century, although a sign warns that, along with bicycles and skateboards, they are forbidden on the pier.

The end of the pier viewed through the carriages of the little trackless trains which run along the seafront. When the Dotto train first arrived in the 1970s there was an outcry from critics who felt that it lowered the tone.

Carpet gardens, *c.* 1910. They don't stretch very far, but the carpet gardens by the pier have long been major attractions, suggesting both a gentle climate and a pursuit of quality.

Gardening fashions change, but this is still a 'bedding out' paradise. Note the many changes to the buildings facing the sea. Beneath the Burlington Hotel (at the right of the photograph) are the remains of a Roman villa.

Royal Sussex Regiment Memorial. This postcard was sent in 1906, the year that the Duke of Norfolk unveiled the memorial to men 'who lost ther lives during the service of the Battalion abroad in Malta, Egypt and in India from 1882 to 1902, and in special memory of the campaigns in which the battalion took part, the Black Mountain Expedition of 1888 and the Tirah Campaign of 1897/8.' Dreadful to think that the young lad giving the proud salute was almost certain to be caught up in a far more bloody conflict as soon as he came of age.

The scene is little changed today, with the terrace on the left in Cavendish Place looking very well cared for. The social and political philosopher Friedrich Engels often stayed at no. 2. When he died, his ashes were scattered at Beachy Head, with Karl Marx's widow in attendance.

Elms Avenue runs up towards Cavendish Place and the sea, and it has changed little over the years. With their verandahs and wide porches, the houses on the left have the faintest feel of New Orleans about them. Who the bearded gentleman was I have no idea: it was impossible to find a modern equivalent of his stylish, but probably none too comfortable, hired carriage.

Queen's Hotel. Jutting out across the promenade, the building was designed by the Duke of Devonshire's architect, Henry Currey, to divide the swank of Grand Parade from the less genteel Marine Parade with its smaller hotels and boarding houses. It opened in 1888. Today the hotel is little changed externally, but the road now sweeps past it where once pedestrians had the thoroughfare all to themselves.

Marine Parade, *c.* 1905. The Albion Hotel, in the centre of the picture, was originally built in 1821 as the private residence of Lord Ashburnham. It was later not only the first hotel in the town to have electricity, but the first to possess a telephone – with the number Eastbourne 1, of course. On the left of the picture is Sea Houses, one of the original hamlets in the borough. Charles Darwin stayed in one of the houses while writing *On the Origin of Species*.

The main photograph on page 72 has a sign pointing round the corner to the library, and here it is – Gowland's in Sea Houses, with the legend 'Library and Reading Rooms' on the awning.

The Albion Hotel has become the Carlton, and has been completely reconstructed inside. Otherwise, the cars make most of the difference.

Sea Houses, *c.* 1890. This is the view looking west, with an Albion Hotel very different in appearance to its later manifestation. Note the winches on the beach for dragging boats ashore.

There are a good many changes today, not least the superstructure of the pier filling in the middle distance. The Carlton Hotel (formerly the Albion) is on the right.

Angles Private Pension, 1925. 'Happy days at Angles' reads the slogan under this photograph of relaxed, predominantly young, holidaymakers. The boarding house was situated on Royal Parade – at the less sumptuous end of the seafront.

Today this is the Majestic Hotel, its ground floor verandah now protected from the elements by glass.

The Kynance Hotel lay a little to the east of the Angles (see previous page) and was altogether smaller. Now it has been turned into flats. 'Successfully let', reads an agent's sign.

Redoubt shelter, *c.* 1909. The dashing foam was a regular hazard or pleasure here: it was clearly pleasant to relax on the front by the Redoubt fortress in days gone by. The Great Redoubt was built in Napoleonic times as a command fort linked with the chain of small, but incredibly stout, martello towers installed along the coast of eastern Sussex.

The brickwork at the top left fixes the position, but there is little to attract the visitor to this neglected spot today. Fortunately the Redoubt tea gardens are only a few steps away. Note how the drifting shingle has now banked up against the promenade.

Crumbles Tramway, *c.* 1955. Beyond Prince's Park, at the eastern end of Royal Parade, there was once little but the shingle of the Crumbles. A tramway, unusually using double-decker cars, ran along here on a 2ft gauge track.

All signs of the tramway have long since gone. The Crumbles themselves have virtually disappeared under developments such as the Sovereign Centre and Sovereign Harbour (see page 125).

5

Along Seaside

Fishmongers, 252 Seaside Road, *c.* 1905. Sadly a change in the numbering system along Seaside Road makes it impossible to pinpoint these premises. Local fish was a speciality for J.T. Colstick, but the shop sold eggs and game, too.

Eastbourne Water Company, Trinity Trees, 1902. The Edwardian age is being welcomed in with a flourish at the offices of the waterworks company. The flags and portraits celebrate the new king's coronation. The uniformed young man on the left appears to be delivering a telegram.

Alas, a very drab sight today, and no room for flags anywhere should the occasion arise.

Seaside Road, *c.* 1920. Despite garage signs on both sides of the street, there isn't a car in sight in this busy shopping area. Awnings were a common feature, keeping out the heat as well as rain.

The buildings on the immediate left have changed, but otherwise the scene is similar – and there are even a few small awnings to be seen.

Chapmans, Victoria Place, *c.* 1905. The top end of Terminus Road from the junction of Trinity Trees and Seaside Road was formerly known as Victoria Place, and here Chapman and Sons had their head office. This picture shows charabancs ready to leave for an outing. The shop on the far corner is Dale & Kerley, drapers and milliners.

Dale & Kerley is now T.J. Hughes and is much changed, while the Chapman building has disappeared altogether: the new building houses the Qualisea Fish Restaurant and Take Away.

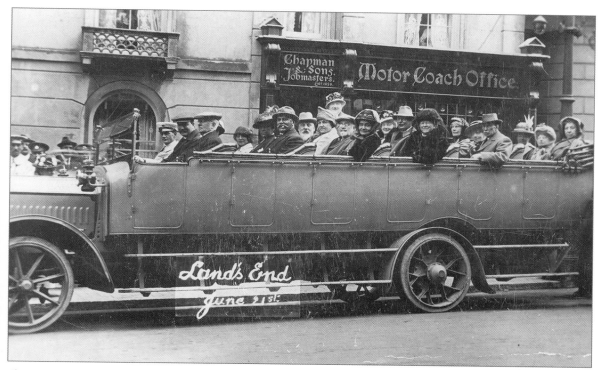

Chapmans put their first motor vehicle into service in 1909, and in 1923 they made motoring history, according to the *Eastbourne Gazette*, by being the first company to conduct a complete tour, organising not only the transport but the hotel accommodation, too. The historic journey (pictured above) was to Land's End.

'One lady, who has crossed the Atlantic several times, stated that being on a motor coach with a party like the one which visited Land's End was like taking a trip over to America by one of the great liners. Everyone was so sociable, and every detail had been well thought out.'

The return journey was about 660 miles, and the driver, Mr F.W. Taylor, was highly praised: 'The passengers presented him with a purse containing a substantial amount.'

Royal Victoria Sea Water Baths, *c.* 1905. The baths were at the top end of Victoria Place, near Grand Parade, and were fed by seawater at every tide. An advertisement of 1877 boasted that the baths were 'replete with every requisite', including Royal porcelain, and that their construction ensured 'strict privacy and cleanliness'. The cart outside belonged to the London, Brighton and South Coast Railway.

This area was bombed during the war, and the baths are lost without trace. The building on the other side of Burlington Road is now a fish and omelette house.

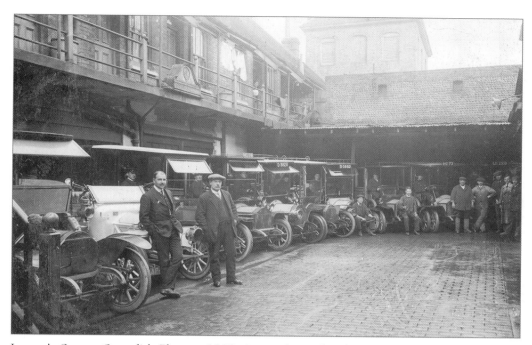

Jermyn's Garage, Cavendish Place, *c.* 1910. As we observed earlier, garages seem to have been a feature of the Seaside Road area. This one, just round the corner in Cavendish Place, is well stocked with sturdy roadsters.

Garage life staggered on here into the twenty-first century, but only just. In the summer of 2001 the site was being sold for redevelopment.

The Tivoli Cinema, Seaside Road, *c.* 1985. Here we see the cinema still clinging to life as a performing arts centre after a chequered career. In 1879, when this was the Mutual Improvement Society's hall, the top floor was used for cinematographic shows. From the Eastbourne Cinema Picture Palace in 1912 it became the Tivoli Cinema in 1915, and later an arts centre and a night club. The parade of shops next door looks sturdy enough, but while workmen were renovating it in April 1994 the building suddenly collapsed, debris spilling across the road and narrowly missing a passing bus.

Later the cinema became Shimmers Leisure Centre and Carrington's Club, but by late 2001 the sale signs were up. The building next door (The Housing Corporation: 'Residential units for rent') is new, but has echoes of what was there before.

Jolliffe & Son, Susans Road, *c.* 1930. This is one of those photographs that repays attention with a magnifying glass. The window is packed with decorating equipment and advertisements: 'English wallpapers bring nature's perfect colour indoors.' Wonderful tosh.

Bomb damage removed a long row of houses here, but No. 19 was (unimaginatively) rebuilt as the headquarters of Eastbourne Liberal Club. Today it's the home of Mobile Phone City.

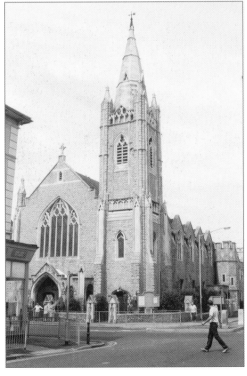

Stone-laying, Central Methodist Church, 1907. It's Easter Monday, and the crowds are out in force for the launch of a new Methodist church on the corner of Pevensey Road with Susans Road. A great picture – but one feels sorry for the young lad crammed into his white suit over on the left.

It must have been a tempting landmark for German bombers, but the church now approaches its centenary as an imposing fixture in the landscape.

Opening of Centre Wesleyan Hall & Schools, 1907. Several faces in the photograph on page 86 reappear here, and that's no surprise: this is the back of the Methodist complex, at the Langney Road end.

The Great Missionary Exhibition photograph, taken outside the Wesleyan hall, is an engaging curiosity. 'This is two of the horses I bought from Daddy,' explains the writer of the postcard in 1909.

Pevensey Road, *c.* 1905. A view from the Susans Road end of the street shows 'tea and dining rooms' on the left, among a parade of small shops. The terrace on the right, conversely, has only one shop among its fairly substantial houses.

Little has changed today, save for the nature of the shops themselves. The street is now one-way and narrowed at the end.

Dashwood & Son, *c.* 1930. A clearly flourishing business on the corner of Pevensey Road with Susans Road, diametrically opposite the Methodist church. A van of that size presumably required a few runs in order to move a complete house of furniture. The small opening on the right leads down to a second-hand furniture display in the basement.

Today it is a restaurant, just glimpsed in the corner of the photograph on the opposite page.

Pevensey Road, *c.* 1905. The upper end of the road was purely residential. The milkman is on his rounds, the little cart stocked with a large churn and pouring jugs.

So little has changed that, amazingly, that gap between the houses on the right still hasn't been filled in. Very lax of the developers.

Confectioners' shop, Seaside Road *c.* 1910. A wonderful display on the corner of Seaside with Belnore Road, Dr Allinson's wholemeal bread being a particular attraction. Fry's Chocolate, which appears in so many photographs of the period, is given characteristic prominence, too.

This is one of those uncomfortable contrasts, the replacement building being uncompromisingly dull. An estate agent now occupies the site, with a newsagent next door rather than a jeweller.

Leaf Hall, Seaside *c.* 1905. What the above gathering represents it is now impossible to say, but let's hope it was something suitably uplifting. William Leaf donated the money for this building in 1864, its purpose being to provide working men with a leisure centre and so keep them out of the pubs. (Not as easy as it sounds: when the Salvation Army attempted to cure people of their vice there were serious riots.) At the time this photograph was taken it was the Leaf Hall Social Institute, with a lending library and rooms for hire. Today the building has a variety of uses, serving among other things as the headquarters of Eastbourne Karate Club.

Salvation Army citadel, Langney Road. It's surprising to discover that the Sally Army's HQ wasn't always as much a fortress in appearance as today. The top photograph was taken around 1980, before a new frontage was added and the turrets were rather jauntily embellished. Although widely respected today, the Army was subjected to vilification in 1891 when several of its members were imprisoned for marching in the streets with music. What really annoyed the locals was General Booth's opposition to the demon drink, and there was rioting in the streets.

Baker & White's, Seaside, *c.* 1908. This well stocked clothing and furniture store stood on the corner of Carlton Road, a long way down the street from the town centre. The whole parade looks prosperous, with a tobacconist next door and then a fruiterer.

A cigarette advertisement has replaced the shop sign. Will future generations think it odd that the dangers of the product are given such prominence? This photograph was taken on a Sunday when the shops were closed, but they undeniably have less character than their predecessors.

6

The Old Town

Motcombe Gardens, *c.* 1925.

Ocklynge Road, *c.* 1930. We approach the Old Town by turning down Ocklynge Road from Willingdon Road – just as the stagecoaches did in days gone by. The tower of St Mary's church can be seen above the rooftops in the centre of the picture.

... the same today, although some of the original houses further down the road ...d.

Ocklynge Road again. This is the view looking back up the road from a little lower down. It must have taken some strength and determination to haul that cart in the older photograph up the slope.

Ocklynge Road, looking towards Crown Street, *c.* 1910. This is deep in the Old Town, with the church up behind us to our left. A faded advertisement on the near wall advertises the Star Brewery, which stood very close to here on what is now the Safeway site. Conservationists almost managed to save this historic building in the 1970s, but the developers demolished it days before the necessary protection was put in place.

Some of the buildings remain, including what is now the post office, but the changes are nonetheless substantial. Brodie Close on the right remembers the Revd Alexander Brodie, who came to Eastbourne in 1809 as vicar of St Mary's and was fatally injured in a carriage accident near the Crown Inn in Crown Street.

Old Post Office, Ocklynge Road, 1865. This delightful old postcard gives an indication of what has been lost in the Old Town. We have only the church to give us a clue as to where these cottages once stood. The subpostmaster then was Mr T. Pain.

Today's photograph is taken from the end of Brodie Close (see opposite). No comment is necessary.

Crown Street was a lively part of the Old Town, although it seems less vital a part of it following the modern developments which have changed the layout of local streets and destroyed many older properties altogether. Many of the buildings closest to the camera remain the same as they were some 90 years ago (a model centre has replaced the draper's), but the church has gone, opening up a view of the Downs.

High Street, Old Town *c.* 1910. The road narrows towards the church, crowded in by shops on either side. The horse-and-carriage is 'parked' close to the bend without the slightest danger of a collision.

The building in the foreground remains, but a swathe has been cut through the buildings on the right, exposing the gable end of the medieval Lamb Inn. On the right, masked by trees, is the Safeway supermarket where once the Star Brewery stood.

High Street, Old Town. Here we have a view further up the street than the photograph on page 101, this one showing more detail of the buildings on the left-hand side. Today's picture shows that a great deal has gone here, too. An arrow points to the Towner Museum & Art Gallery, now occupying the manor house formerly owned by the Gildredge and Gilbert families.

St Mary's churchyard, *c.* 1910. A Baker Sons & Hide bakery van is seen making its leisurely way past the churchyard, with closely packed houses all the way down the street.

Half a house, or so it seems, now stands at the spot the van was passing, and the middle distant view is less pleasantly cluttered. The churchyard itself has been tidied up, too, with several of the gravestones and the tree removed.

St Mary's Parsonage, *c.* 1930. Built as the rectory manor in the sixteenth century, the Old Parsonage was in a neglected state when, in 1912, the Duke of Devonshire bought it, gave it to the parish and donated a generous contribution towards its restoration. At the time of this photograph it was looking sound once again.

Today the building looks much the same, although there are signs of further remedial work in the way of the chimney support and the wall ties. The iron railings around the church have gone, presumably to be melted down for the war effort.

Pilgrims, Borough Lane, *c.* 1935. The postcard boldly describes this as 'the oldest house in Eastbourne', but a plaque on the wall is a little more restrained. Romantics like to imagine long tunnels linking the cellars of buildings such as this, and the Lamb Inn across the road has a very atmospheric undercroft, but the evidence is usually lacking.

The street name has been moved, and a notice has been erected to keep unnecessary lorries away, but otherwise there is little change but for the sprouting television aerials.

Motcombe Gardens, *c.* 1910. We are here at the still heart of Eastbourne. The early settlement grew up around the spring which feeds this pond and whose waters flow (as the Bourne stream) to the sea. The farm yard of Motcombe Farm – one of whose buildings can be seen on the left of the photograph – came to the edge of the pond, which then spread over a wider area than now and probably lapped the footings of the flint dovecote nearby. Our photograph captures the tranquil nature of this little retreat.

There has been a good deal of change beyond the park. The farm building has gone, and so has the house immediately beyond the gate, which was home to a boot repairer in the above picture. In the house immediately to its right lived the comedian Tommy Cooper.

Motcombe Gardens, 1954. The date is 31 January, and the pond is frozen, forcing the gulls to congregate on the one clear patch of moving water. Behind are Motcombe Baths, with their tall chimneys.

The greenery has grown substantially, but otherwise the view is largely unchanged today.

Tally-Ho, *c.* 1905. A rare picture of this Old Town pub, at the junction of Church Street with Green Street, in its earlier and more sedate guise. There is no hanging sign outside, although the painting of a hunted fox appears on the wall. The steps on the left of the photograph led up to St Mary's Hospital, which was pulled down in 1990.

The present, somewhat sprawling, building has stood on the site for some 70 years. A mounted huntsman and his dog grace the sign, while Sheila's Steakhouse is a fairly new attraction. Note how much wider Green Street has become at this point.

19 Green Street,
c. 1935. George
Thomas stands proudly
outside the business he
called Hospital for Sick
Boots. The entrance of
No. 19 is, in fact, just
round the corner in
Okehurst Road.

The house is structurally unchanged, but it has lost some of its workaday quality. The brick paving has given way to concrete, and the door and windowframes are tasteful hardwood replacements.

Empire Day, Green Street, 1913. It is the year before 'the war to end all wars', and the boys of St Mary's school, with their parents in attendance, are gathered under the Union Jack to celebrate Empire Day. The photograph was taken from Dacre Street, with Green Street running across the background.

The school has gone, to be replaced by Wyke House, a large and well-proportioned block of flats for the elderly.

Victoria Drive, *c.* 1915. A view from the corner of Okehurst Road towards Willingdon and the Downs. The tall stack in the distance is a sewer vent.

The road is no wider today, despite the much heavier traffic – and we would still see that sewer vent but for the maturity of the trees.

East Dean Road, *c.* 1920. Trotting in the middle of the road was no problem eighty years ago. This is the view out of the Old Town up the East Dean Road, with the Downs as a backdrop. The unmade road shows evidence that other horses have already passed this way.

Remarkable continuity, with even the low flint walls surviving. The line of houses has, of course, marched further up the road.

7

The Meads Area

Meads Road, *c.* 1905.

Paradise Drive, *c.* 1905. The name might be chosen to invite ridicule, but was there a more pleasant spot in Eastbourne to drive your horse and cart? The road winds around the edge of the Royal Eastbourne Golf Course, on the lower ground to the left, before descending into the Meads area.

The blur of the car in the foreground explains the safety fencing installed on the bend, but we are recognisably at the same spot. Even the little kink in the road remains where that tree stump stands in the older picture: it makes a convenient refuge for a photographer's car.

Meads Road, *c.* 1910. Another way to Meads is out of the town centre via the town hall. This photograph was taken just up the road from there at the junction with Compton Place Road. Compton Place was the home of the Earl of Burlington, and hence the 'operations room' for the development of Eastbourne when he became Duke of Devonshire.

The house on the left is still there, but the road is wider now, and all the houses on the right are modern.

Meads Road, *c.* 1905. This is the length of Meads Road above Carlisle Road which has long been a dual carriageway, although the left-hand side was originally meant to be a service road for the mansions which fronted it. If that suggests speed, however, the positioning of the tree and the lamppost offer a sharp corrective.

The shape of the road is identical today, but the impediments to speedy motoring have been whisked away.

Meads Village, *c.* 1918. The houses grouped around gardens a little off Meads Street were built for workers on the Compton Estate. In this picture the plots look less than fully developed.

Today the gardens are a delight. Some are given over to flowers and some to vegetables, while others are bowery retreats with mature shrubs and fruit trees. Miss Louise Collins, seen on the left, was born in her house in 1912, and she has tended her garden since she was ten years old.

The Pilot Inn, Meads *c.* 1930. A delivery from the Star Brewery to a pub which was quenching thirsts before modern Eastbourne was created. The pub name was apparently mounted on the roof so that it would be visible for a considerable distance to travellers approaching over the Downs.

Eating is as important as drinking in most modern pubs, and here people are tucking in to the Pilot's ploughman's lunches.

Holywell, *c.* 1905. King Edward's Parade continues west past Meads from Grand Parade, and in 1905 the Holywell Retreat was laid out below it in a former chalk pit. This postcard was sent in 1907, when this was still a novelty.

In 1922 the spot was converted into the Holywell Italian Gardens, and some of the atmospheric columns can be glimpsed above the vegetation. The path from above into the gardens is now screened by greenery, but the lower path down the low chalk cliff has been eroded.

Ice cream seller, Dukes Drive, 1928. King Edward's Parade in turn becomes Dukes Drive as it swings under the inland slopes of Beachy Head, and here in the 1920s Charles Wilson (a wheelwright by trade) used to sell ices from his car. The rugs draped over the wheels were presumably to protect the rubber tyres from the heat.

A permanent ice cream kiosk stands at the same spot today. Mr Wilson obviously started something.

8

Further Afield

Park Lane, Hampden Park *c.* 1905. This rural retreat, which runs between Willingdon Road and King's Drive, is more built-up today, with Ratton School part of the way along it, but it still has an off-the-beaten-track feel.

Beachy Head and the lighthouse. The lighthouse has appeared on countless postcards since its beam first swept the sea in October 1902, but the ever-crumbling cliff means that the view is constantly changing.

The effects of a particularly dramatic fall in 1998 can still be seen in the bottom picture. The newly fallen chalk is gradually being smoothed by the elements, and the lighthouse is at present much closer to the shore than it was in the earlier photograph taken some 50 years before.

Beachy Head Hotel, *c.* 1935. The wind can be brisk and very cold on Beachy Head, and this group appears to be making the best of a bad job. The first hotel here was the Queen's, but it burned down in the 1920s – a fate which was to befall two further hotels on the spot.

The modern Beachy Head Hotel is very much a family restaurant, with a children's playground next to it and an adjoining wildlife interpretation centre.

Langney Priory, Etchingham Road. 'This is a very old house', wrote the sender of the above postcard in 1938. 'We have been all over it and round the garden. Stayed and had tea on the lawn.' Part of the building is pre-Conquest, including a chapel with a Saxon archway, and it was developed at various stages from the fourteenth to the sixteenth centuries. Today the priory is in private hands, and somewhat difficult to find in the middle of a housing estate.

The Crumbles. The Crumbles once extended miles to the east of Eastbourne – lonely shingle banks stretching to Pevensey Bay, and a home to breeding birds and salt-loving plants. Most of it has gone today, and the greatest incursion on its solitude has been the building of the Sovereign Harbour, a vast and highly popular marina.

Rodmill Farm. Fortunately not all change is as drastic as this. The main photograph shows Rodmill Farm, with Willingdon church in the top right corner fixing the position. In recent times the farm has completely disappeared. Today's picture shows the Rodmill roundabout in King's Drive, close to Eastbourne District General Hospital, with new housing spread over the old farmland.

ACKNOWLEDGEMENTS

I am not a collector of photographs and postcards, and so am grateful beyond measure to the people who have lent me the material in this book. The bulk of it comes from three collectors. Robert Armstrong, author of (among other titles) *Robert Armstrong's Eastbourne*, is an old friend who, apart from giving me so many good pictures, piloted me around the town to point out features which I would have been hard pressed to find myself. Des Puttock and Nigel Steer have been all the more remarkable in their generosity in that I had never met either of them before. I should add that the captions I have written are my own work entirely, and that any errors I may have made are no reflection on the knowledge of these three kind men, without whom the book would not have appeared at all.

I had other help, too. Several readers of the local newspaper responded to my request for illustrative material, sometimes sending me their precious photographs in the post by way of introduction. I thank them all, and especially those whose postcards and photographs I have been able to reproduce: Gordon Clark (to whom I am also indebted for sharing his deep knowledge of Eastbourne), Mrs J.A. Taylor, Mrs J.F. Hacker, Mrs P. Thumwood, Mrs Joan Maynard and Ray Tingley. I should further like to thank Tony Chamberlain-Brothers for his typically shy and retiring pose in his town crier's uniform, and the Towner Art Gallery and Museum for permission to reproduce the postcard on page 98.

This book is compiled by an experienced Primary School teacher and covers much of the National Curriculum work your child will be doing at school.

Make sure your child understands each page before he or she begins the exercise. Extra paper and pens, pencils or crayons are useful. These are NOT 'Tests' and working with you, using an encyclopedia, a calculator or a dictionary, will be very helpful.

Don't do too much at a time and try to ensure that your child has a feeling of SUCCESS!

(Answers at the back of the book.)

First edition

Published by Ladybird Books Ltd Loughborough Leicestershire UK
Ladybird Books Inc Auburn Maine 04210 USA

© LADYBIRD BOOKS LTD MCMXCII
All rights reserved. No part of this publication may be reproduced, stored in a retrieval system, or transmitted in any form or by any means, electronic, mechanical, photocopying, recording or otherwise, without the prior consent of the copyright owner.

Printed in England (7)